SEVEN WAYS TO KNOW IF SHE LOVES YOU

WHAT EVERY GUY SHOULD KNOW

JAY JANDY

Table of Contents

INTRODUCTION

Finding the right woman who truly loves you, is one of the biggest fears a guy has. Trying to make sure he's not been played or taken for granted or something of that nature.

Now in this read, I have highlighted some salient points that should be noted, although they are not exhaustible.

Falling in love is a very good thing, but to be loved in return, the feeling is indescribable!

Want to know these signs? Check it out then.

Enjoy!

CHAPTER ONE

Sustains Conversation

If she loves you, she should be able to keep the conversation going. Not like that of a chatter box per say, but she finds something interesting about you or something to keep the flow of conversation. Sometimes it could be that "sweet nothingness" between lovers who are obsessed with each other.

If both of you are distant in location from each other, whatever form of communication y'll choose to use, it should be daily. And if she only responds only when you send her a message or call her, you have to think twice about her love for you. Because love being mutual, she should feel the same enthusiasm as you feel to want to talk to you, not only when you initiate the conversation.

INTENTIONALLY LEFT BLANK

INTENTIONALLY LEFT BLANK

INTENTIONALLY LEFT BLANK

CHAPTER TWO

Compliments

When in love with someone, it is absolutely important that compliments are given and taken. You cannot claim you love someone and don't compliment him at all, even when you can see that he's all cute and stuff or does things for you which you know only love could have inspired such deeds.

Compliments actually makes you feel good right? So if she doesn't give it, bro!

A lady in love with you would seize every opportunity to give you compliments, especially if she knows it makes you feel better coming from her.

INTENTIONALLY LEFT BLANK

INTENTIONALLY LEFT BLANK

INTENTIONALLY LEFT BLANK

CHAPTER THREE

She Hides You

When women are in love, they are so eager to talk to their friends about it as well as their family members. Well maybe not tell the family members everything (just in case the relationship goes south) but at least they know she's in love with someone.

So if she keeps hiding you from her friends, most especially her family, bro she's not in love with you, neither is she proud to be your woman. The earlier you realize it the better for you.

Any woman truly in love with you, wants to show you off to the world, except it's a mutual agreement between both of you.

INTENTIONALLY LEFT BLANK

CHAPTER FOUR

Jealousy

Men are jealous about who they love, and so also are women.

If she doesn't feel any iota of jealousy about you talking to or in the company of other ladies, that's a sign she doesn't care about her love for you.

A woman who truly loves you will want to guard her territory from other "intruders" from taking her man. It's just a natural thing to protect what you love from any intrusion. No one is lackadaisical about what they hold dear. How do you feel when another guy is talking to your woman? You feel a pinch of jealousy right? That's how she should feel, for a woman who loves you.

INTENTIONALLY LEFT BLANK

CHAPTER FIVE

Sacrifices

A woman who loves you would make sacrifices for you.

She will voluntarily do a lot of stuff for you because it's from her heart. You wouldn't need to force her or give her clues of what she should do. She's just inspired by her love for you.

She wouldn't want to see you suffer or go through anything alone.

In other words, she wants to make your burden light, if not totally taking it away. So if she's not doing this, well, you have another signal to tell you that she…

INTENTIONALLY LEFT BLANK

CHAPTER SIX

She Loves Your Company

When a woman love you, she will always want to be in your company. She will be interested in you and also want to know more about you.

Her facial expressions shows how happy she is being around you.

This can lead to both of you doing some silly childish things together without being ashamed or embarrassed whatsoever.

If she doesn't love you, she will always look for ways to avoid your company and going to events with you. For those in love, usually 24hours is usually not enough to love up. Trust me on this.

INTENTIONALLY LEFT BLANK

INTENTIONALLY LEFT BLANK

INTENTIONALLY LEFT BLANK

CHAPTER SEVEN

Vibes Over Words

Any day anytime and anywhere, its vibes over words. What's vibes? Simply put, Energy!

How much words she says doesn't matter as much as the energy she uses to carry them out or display what she has said.

It's more of a "Walk-the-talk" kind of thing you understand?

Vibes don't lie, somehow you will feel it. It's that contagious if you're sensitive enough to feel it.

When she truly loves you, her vibes will show clearly. Her enthusiastic energy will be felt miles away. No wonder it's easy to tell when a lady is truly in love with someone, she can't stop talking about him and all that.

INTENTIONALLY LEFT BLANK

CHAPTER EIGHT

CONCLUSION

If after these few tips you're not still able to tell if she really loves you, then wow! But essentially it's easy to tell though, going with the flow of it. What I've basically said so far is that, any lady in love, cannot hide it, it will show! One way or another.

Do have a happily-ever-after ☺

www.ingramcontent.com/pod-product-compliance
Lightning Source LLC
LaVergne TN
LVHW052115160826
845678LV00015B/3577

* 9 7 9 8 8 4 8 1 6 9 8 8 1 *